FEAR OF
MUSIC

by Barney Norris

Published by Playdead Press 2013

© Barney Norris

Barney Norris has asserted his rights under the
Copyright, Design and Patents Act, 1988, to be
identified as the author of this work.

A CIP catalogue record for this book is available from
the British Library.

ISBN 978-0-9575266-1-7

Playdead Press
www.playdeadpress.com

For Joz.

With thanks to everyone who has contributed to the development of this play, particularly the company of *Missing*, Frank and Elizabeth Brenan, Arts Council England, Out of Joint and above all to Alice.

Up In Arms

www.upinarms.org.uk

@upinarmstheatre

"There is clearly lots of talent in the young Up In Arms theatre group" Whatsonstage.com

"Critically acclaimed production company Up In Arms" British Theatre Guide

Artistic Directors: Alice Hamilton and Barney Norris

Producer: Chloe Courtney

Patrons: Peter Gill and David Hare

Education Manager: Ashleigh Wheeler

Webmaster: Jake Anders

Associate Designer: Matthew Ward

Supported using public funding by
ARTS COUNCIL ENGLAND
LOTTERY FUNDED

out of joint

LOTTERY FUNDED

Supported using public funding by
**ARTS COUNCIL
ENGLAND**

Inquisitive, epic, authentic and original: Out of Joint is a national and international touring theatre company, developing entertaining theatre that broadens horizons and investigates our times.

"You expect something special from Out of Joint" The Times
"Inventive, individual and humane" Whatsonstage.com

Under the direction of Max Stafford-Clark the company has premiered plays from leading writers including April De Angelis, Sebastian Barry, Richard Bean, Alistair Beaton, Caryl Churchill, David Hare, Robin Soans and Timberlake Wertenbaker, as well as launching first-time writers such as Mark Ravenhill and Stella Feehily. Recent revivals include the West End-transferring *Top Girls*; and its acclaimed new production of *Our Country's Good*, at the new St James Theatre until March 2013.

Out of Joint frequently performs at and co-produces with key venues such as the Royal Court and the National Theatre and dynamic regional theatres such as the Octagon Theatre Bolton, and has performed in six continents. The company also pursues an extensive education programme.

ONLINE BOOKSHOP
Buy play scripts and other books at discounted prices from our website.

KEEP IN TOUCH – JOIN OUR MAILING LIST
www.outofjoint.co.uk | ojo@outofjoint.co.uk | 020 7609 0207
Twitter: @out_of_joint | Facebook: "Out of Joint theatre company"

Forgotten People

Barney Norris on rewrites, the army, and the strange fame of Andover.

In 2008 I was in a play called *Through the Leaves* by the German writer Franz Xaver Kroetz, in a production directed by Alice Hamilton, the director of *Fear Of Music*. I hadn't previously encountered Kroetz, Germany's most frequently performed living playwright, and his work fascinated me. I thought *Through The Leaves* was incredible: a portrait of a failed affair between a butcher and a roaming drunk (that was me) that put life on stage and demanded we pay it attention. I thought, I want to write a play like that. I'd just written my first short play, a piece called *At First Sight* about the memory of a failed affair, which was very romantic, and wanted to try something different. This uncompromising portrait of real life, not commenting, just showing, struck me as an exciting model.

The story of *Fear Of Music* started with two ideas. Firstly, I thought I could write about the experience of sharing a bedroom with your brother; secondly, I wanted to explore an image Alice's mother Jane had put in my head. Jane told me that on the day she had moved out of her childhood home, the last time she looked into the kitchen, she had seen herself and her family five years earlier in the room – not remembered it, but seen the memory taking place in front of her eyes. I thought that was an amazing trigger for a play, so I wrote about two brothers refracted through the lens of memory. Alice didn't think it was very good. I did a workshop and a reading and discovered she was right. The play went on the back burner, a story without impetus I put in a drawer.

Then, in 2010, I walked past an army recruitment poster that said 'this is my life: I want to do more with it than flip burgers', and knew at once that I had to go home and get back to writing. The slogan struck me as an incredibly offensive piece of bullying – a targeted belittling by the state. The idea that the Army marketing department might play on the insecurities of ordinary people suffering from a lack of opportunity in order to put them in the line of fire seemed abhorrent: so I went home and wrote another layer into my story. I organised another reading, and Alice and I began to plan a production.

I'm cautious about sounding rabidly anti-army. This November 11th the company of *Fear Of Music* went to the Remembrance Day service in Andover, where the play is set. We were struck by the beauty of the idea the army presented of itself at that ceremony, which strikes me as the central ritual of our society (it seems to me that England in the last century has been, above all, a story about the war). My grandfather lost three brothers in the Great War, and still lives a hundred metres from the memorial where their names are inscribed. The sacrifices made by soldiers for my life are woven into my family's identity, and at that level, the level of the individual soldier, I feel conscious of a tremendous debt to the people who make up the army. But my argument wasn't with them. The army is an arm of the state – and it's a failure of our state if, rather than working to improve conditions for those on low incomes or in deprived areas, we exploit their insecurities and aggress them into barracks, a systematic practise documented by Forces Watch:

http://www.forceswatch.net/what_why. It's feudal.

I hadn't known at first that I wanted to set the play in Andover. But then the Tories got into power and in late 2010, while I was working at the Bush Theatre, announced new benefit caps for families. People I knew on benefits in Shepherds Bush just laughed at these: there was no way a family could live on that in that area. I learned that on the day these caps had been announced, Hammersmith and Fulham council had block-booked B&Bs across Brentford for the weeks following the date the new rates were due to come into effect. They weren't aloof or disconnected; they had done the maths, and knew families on benefits would have to leave the area. It was planned social cleansing, ideological violence.

I wanted to engage with this, but I didn't want to write about 'now'. Seamus Heaney has said that at the height of the Troubles, he and his contemporaries avoided writing about the situation around them because such an attempt tended to produce what he called 'Troubles trash'. I felt like I read and saw a lot of 'banking trash' being made around me too. So I looked for a time when what I wanted to write about – the shuffling of the working class out of city centres, a receding jobs market, a lack of opportunity, a sense of powerlessness, the overpowering shadow of the city on the lives of the people around me – had also been relevant. And I ended up looking at Thatcher.

Andover became the setting because I grew up there and could do the accent; because it's a military town, a natural setting for this story, and because during the 80s Andover became a battleground for the abnegation of social responsibility. From the 60s, the London Overspill

5

relocations project transformed Andover from a town of 5,000 to one of 50,000. Facing overcrowding in the metropolis, the GLC paid to turn places like Andover into overspill towns, and relocated people in social housing out to the country. In Andover, this wasn't the end of the story: by the 80s, it was clear the new housing was so badly built it would have to be done again. Andover Council got a lot of coverage when it had to bring a suit against the GLC before they made a settlement to pay for this second draft of the new town. Nowhere was it more painfully clear how unwanted the public were by the state. So that seemed like a good place to write a play about forgotten people.

Fear of Music was first presented by Up In Arms with the support of Out of Joint at York Theatre Royal on February 19th, 2013 with the following cast:

Luke - Hasan Dixon

Andy- Jack Finch

Writer - Barney Norris

Director - Alice Hamilton

Designer - Carys Rose Beard

Lighting Designer - Simon Gethin Thomas

Sound Designer - Tom Gibbons

Stage Manager - Charlie Young

This script was accurate at the time of going to print but may have changed during rehearsals.

TOUR DATES

19-20 February York Theatre Royal
01904 623 568 | www.yorktheatreroyal.co.uk

25-26 February Hull Truck Theatre
01482 323 638 | www.hulltruck.co.uk

27 February South Shields Customs House
01914 541 234 | www.customshouse.co.uk

28 Feb – 2 March London Tristan Bates Theatre
0207 240 6283 | www.tristanbatestheatre.co.uk

11-13 March Oxford Playhouse
01865 305 305 | www.oxfordplayhouse.com

14 March Andover James's Place
01264 772 400 | www.james-place.co.uk

19-20 March Ipswich High School for Girls
01473 780 201 | www.ipswichhigh.gdst.net

22 March Middlesbrough Theatre
01642 815 181 | www.middlesbroughtheatre.co.uk

25-26 March Salisbury Playhouse
01722 320 333 | www.salisburyplayhouse.com

27 March Norden Farm Arts Centre
01628 788 997 | www.nordenfarm.org

COMPANY

Hasan Dixon | Luke

Training: Central School of Speech and Drama.
Theatre includes: *The Alchemist* (Liverpool playhouse); *The Glass Menagerie* (Everyman Theatre); *You The Player* (West Yorkshire Playhouse/Look Left Look Right); *Stand Up Diggers All!* (Pentabus); *Yerma* (Gate/Hull Truck); *Ghosts* (UK tour); *Word Play, Boars and Dragonflies, The Spanish Tragedy* (Arcola); *The Return* (Southwark Playhouse); *The Little Prince* (Exeter Bike Shed); *None But Friends* (Rose Theatre); *'A' Straight* (Undeb); *Publishing A Piece* (BAC); *The Jungle Book* (Birmingham Stage Company). Television includes: *Silent Witness, A Touch of Frost, Doctors*. Film includes: *John Carter, Coincidence*.

Jack Finch | Andy

Jack is in his final year at Central School of Speech and Drama. This is his professional stage debut.

CREATIVE TEAM

Barney Norris | Writer

Barney's plays are *At First Sight* and *Fear Of Music*. His first pamphlet of poems, *Falling*, has just been published, and his first book, *To Bodies Gone: The Theatre of Peter Gill*, is forthcoming from Seren. He works at Out of Joint as assistant to Max Stafford-Clark and acts regularly as assistant to Peter Gill.

9

Alice Hamilton | Director

Alice's productions for Up In Arms include *At First Sight* (tour and Latitude Festival) and *Missing* (Tristan Bates Theatre). Other directing includes: *Belarus* (Arcola Theatre for The Miniaturists). She was casting director on *Bloody Poetry* (Jermyn Street Theatre, 2012) and *Shiverman* (Theatre 503, 2012), and assistant director on the *Agamemnon* (Oxford Playhouse, 2008) *Step 9 (of 12)* (Trafalgar Studios, 2012) *Sappho… In Nine Fragments* (Greenwich Theatre, 2012) and *Tu I Teraz* (Hampstead Theatre, Southampton Nuffield and Colchester Mercury, 2012-13). Forthcoming engagements include: assistant director on *A Day In The Death Of Joe Egg* (Rose Theatre/Liverpool Playhouse).

Carys Rose Beard | Designer

Carys trained at Royal Welsh College of Music and Drama. Theatre as designer includes: I Am England (Egg Theatre Bath), The Strange Disappearance of a Lady Parachutist (Chapter Arts, Cardiff), The Get Together (Sherman Theatre Cardiff), The Best Years of your Life (nabokov), O Go My Man (RWCMD). Other theatre includes Branches: The Nature of Crisis (National Theatre Wales, design assistant), Wicked (Apollo Theatre, costume runner), The King's Speech (Germany, costume maker). Film as designer includes: A Welshman's Guide to Breaking Up. carysbeard.wix.com/designer

Simon Gethin Thomas | Lighting Designer

Simon is a London-based designer, and trained for a Master's Degree in Lighting at the Royal Welsh College of Music and Drama. Recent production credits include *Orpheus in the Underworld* (Opera'r Ddraig), *I'd Kill for You: Medea* (Action to the Word), *Revolutionaries in Vienna* (Arensky Chamber Orchestra) and *Blood Wedding* (RWCMD). Previous designs for tours include *Macbeth* (CAST), *Albert Herring* (Shadwell Opera), *The Taming of the Shrew* (CUETG) and *Good For You* (Footlights). For more information, please visit:
www.simongethinthomas.com

Tom Gibbons | Sound Designer

Tom trained at Central School of Speech and Drama and is resident sound designer for the international physical theatre company Parrot{in the}Tank.

Recent design credits include: *Excursions; Just Above The Below; Freeman Gallop*; *Storm out of a Teacup* (Parrot{in the}Tank); *Dead Heavy Fantastic* (Liverpool Everyman); *Plenty* (Sheffield Crucible Studio); *Love Love Love* (Paines Plough, National Tour); *The Machine Gunners* (Polka); *The Chairs* (Theatre Royal, Bath); *The Country; Road To Mecca; The Roman Bath; 1936; The Shawl* (Arcola); *Terror Tales* (Hampstead Studio); *The Hostage; Present Tense* (Southwark Playhouse); *Faustus* (Watford Palace, Tour); *Faithless Bitches* (Courtyard); *The Knowledge; Little Platoons; 50 Ways To Leave Your Lover; 50 Ways To Leave Your Lover@Xmas; Broken Space Season* (Bush Theatre); *Bagpuss; Everything Must Go; Soho Streets* (Soho Theatre); *Holes* (New Wimbledon Studio); *FAT* (The Oval House);

11

Just Me Bell (Graeae, Tour); *Blue Heaven* (Finborough); *Pitching In* (Latitude Festival, Tour); *Overspill; Shape Of Things; Old Man and The Sea; This Limetree Bower; Someone Who'll Watch Over Me* (Cockpit); *US Love Bites* (Old Red Lion, Tristan Bates); *I Can Sing A Rainbow* (Nabokov/Lyceum Sheffield); *Pendulum* (Jermyn Street); *Journalist* and *Hope* (ICA London); *Machinal* (Central); *Bar Of Ideas* (Paradise Gardens Festival and Glastonbury/Shangri-La).

As Associate: *The Aliens* (Bush Theatre)

Charlie Young | Stage Manager

Charlie recently graduated from Middlesex University in Theatre Arts (Design and Technical Theatre). Recent stage management credits include, *The Snail and The Whale* - Tall Stories (Hong Kong, Singapore and UK Tour); *Miss Julie* (Tristan Bates and Edinburgh Fringe); *Jesus Christ Superstar* (Ljubljana, Slovenia); *The Hairy Ape* (Southwark Playhouse) and *Third Floor* (Trafalgar Studios).

CHARACTERS:

LUKE

ANDY, Luke's younger brother.

1

The door bursts open and ANDY rushes in. He slams the door shut behind him and leans against it. He is desperately out of breath. He goes to the window and looks out. He changes out of his clothes and puts on new ones. He stands on the bed to look out of the window. He sits on the bed and holds himself.

2

Night. ANDY is crying in his sleep.

LUKE: Andy. Andy wake up. Hey. Are you all right? [*ANDY gets out of bed. He stands still for a moment, facing LUKE. He is whimpering, as if he might be talking very fast, but there is no suggestion he is saying anything coherent.*] What's wrong mate? [*ANDY tries to get into bed with LUKE.*] What are you doing? No, Andy stop it, no. [*LUKE pushes ANDY away. ANDY keeps trying to get into LUKE'S bed. LUKE gets up to force him away.*] Stop it, please! [*ANDY turns violently away and picks up a bin. He turns and wields it at ANDY.*] Andy. What are you doing? [*ANDY takes a swipe. LUKE gets hold of the bin and takes it off him. ANDY spins away and sits on the floor, sobbing, rocking intensely. LUKE crouches opposite him, putting his hands on ANDY's shoulders.*]

ANDY: I so so so / so so so so so so so so so so so so so so so... fuck you fuck fuck fuck you so so so so...

LUKE: Hey. I'm here, it's OK. It's OK. Can you hear me? Are you asleep? Come on, stop it, you'll wake mum *[ANDY continues whimpering, but quieter now. He does not look at LUKE.]* Can you hear me? Can you wake up?

ANDY: I want...

Silence.

LUKE: Go on. No? Talk to me, Andy, come on. I'm here. I'm here. *[LUKE takes ANDY's right hand in both of his.]* You have to wake up, Andy, it's the middle of the night, this isn't fair. I shouldn't have to do this, you know? Come on. *[He is massaging ANDY's palm, concentrating on it.]* You can't even hear me, this is ridiculous. I'm talking to myself, aren't I. You can't even hear me. *[ANDY withdraws his hand and curls up in a ball on the floor.]* Are you awake? You've gone haven't you? Jesus. Right. *[LUKE picks up ANDY, puts him back in his bed. Pulls the duvet over him.]* If I thought you could hear me - I don't know why someone hasn't killed you yet. Someone will.

LUKE turns away.

ANDY: I want...

16

3

LUKE: When I opened the door I could see us five years ago. I mean, real ghosts, I could hear us. Me and Andy, younger than we are now, sitting on the floor playing toy basketball. Magic Johnson, Michael Jordan. It must have been the smell of the room or the light in the room or something, but I opened the door - and even though it doesn't even look like it did now I saw us sitting right here. We used to spend whole afternoons painting little models, playing board games or fighting. I never let him beat me so he hardly ever won at anything. There's a knot in my stomach I can't ease, and I opened the door and I knew it was in this room. And I can't do anything about it.

4

ANDY is sitting on his bed, playing an unplugged electric guitar. He is not very good, but he's not an absolute beginner.

ANDY: He's going to lend me the AC/DC song book tomorrow.

LUKE: That'll be nice.

ANDY: Shut up, they're brilliant. Aren't they? Aren't they brilliant?

LUKE: Shut up.

ANDY: You shut up. If I'm going to be in a band, I've got to learn to play an instrument.

LUKE: Not for your sort of music. You can't be a rhythm guitarist because you've got no rhythm.

ANDY: When I play Wembley Stadium you'll be talking out the other side of your face, and I still won't be listening to you. I won't be able to hear you, the sound'll go in the wrong direction unless you stand with your back to me.

LUKE: What are you talking about?

ANDY: If you talked out the back of your head.

LUKE: What?

ANDY: You'd have to stand with your back to me.

LUKE: It probably doesn't matter, does it.

ANDY: Depends on whether or not you end up talking out the other side of your face.

LUKE: Is that even a saying?

ANDY: Course it is.

ANDY plays.

LUKE: You're going to be big then, are you?

ANDY: Like Guns n Roses.

LUKE: Come off it.

ANDY: At least like Gary Numan.

LUKE: Gary Numan's better than Guns n Roses.

ANDY: Fuck off.

LUKE: They're both shit.

ANDY: They're not.

LUKE: They are.

ANDY: Shut up.

ANDY plays.

ANDY: We're going to be the best band in the
            world.

LUKE: With a rhythm guitarist who can't clap in
            time.

ANDY: I'm a backing vocalist too.

LUKE: Fine.

ANDY: My main contribution's going to be song
            writing.

LUKE: You can't write songs.

ANDY: I can write songs.

LUKE: You can't.

ANDY: You'll see. [*Plays.*] Can I have your paper
            round when you go?

LUKE: What? All right.

ANDY: I need to buy a guitar. He's only leant me
           this till the end of the week.

LUKE: How much are they?

ANDY: It depends. If you want a Les Paul you
           need hundreds.

LUKE: Do you?

ANDY: Yeah.

LUKE: No, do you want a Les Paul?

ANDY: Yeah. Les Paul Classic. But there might
           not be time. We might start gigging before
           I can save that much.

LUKE: Well you can have my paper round.

ANDY: All right.

LUKE: Don't mention it.

ANDY: Thanks.

ANDY plays.

ANDY: I can't wait till you fuck off.

LUKE: Fuck off.

ANDY: I was just thinking, I could really rock out
            if you weren't here, you know? Really go
            for it.

LUKE: Define 'go for it'.

ANDY: You know. Get some moves out.

LUKE: You can't play it yet, what's the point in
            learning moves?

ANDY: You have to build the moves into your
            style. So you have a unique style. Do you
            feel bad that you're leaving me behind?

LUKE: Why?

ANDY: Rotting in the boondocks. Good name for
            a song.

LUKE: Rotting in the boondocks?

ANDY: Why not?

LUKE: So many reasons. Why aren't you the lead
            singer?

ANDY: Ian's better at it. It's not my kind of
           singing, it makes my throat hurt.

LUKE: Why not be in a band that does your kind
           of singing, and sing?

ANDY: I'm not being in your kind of band. I like
           my music. I'm not being in Crosby,
           fucking and fucking Nash.

LUKE: David Bowie sings, Bryan Ferry sings.

ANDY: It's Ian's band.

LUKE: Then get your own.

ANDY: I can't.

LUKE: You'd do better playing decent music.

ANDY: This is good music.

LUKE: Yeah.

ANDY: It is.

LUKE: Yeah.

ANDY plays.

ANDY: You were never in a band.

LUKE: No.

ANDY: Why not?

LUKE: I didn't have the right friends. You have to be mates with a drummer and a guitarist and a bassist, don't you. I didn't know a drummer.

ANDY: You could still be in one.

LUKE: A band?

ANDY: Yeah. You could still be in one.

LUKE: Yeah.

ANDY: It's not your thing really, is it?

LUKE: Not really, no.

ANDY: I'm not saying you're a loner. I'm not having a go.

LUKE: I didn't say you were.

ANDY: No. You just keep yourself to yourself, don't you?

LUKE: I think more than I talk.

ANDY: I don't talk that much.

LUKE: I didn't say you did.

ANDY: Fine then. We thought we might call
             ourselves 'Living By Vice'.

LUKE: Are you joking?

ANDY: What?

LUKE: You don't live by vice.

ANDY: No, but –

LUKE: You live by your Mum's dole.

ANDY: No –

LUKE: 'Living On Benefits.'

ANDY: 'Friends With Benefits' might be good.

LUKE: No, because everyone would think you and
             Ian were fucking each other.

ANDY: They would not! They'd take one look at
             us and know we were so not. When

Guns'n'Roses tour they don't book hotels. They just pull every night. That'd be me and Ian. Shagged every night.

LUKE: That's a good band name. 'Shagged Every Night.'

ANDY: We thought we might call ourselves 'Fear Of Music.'

LUKE: Seriously?

ANDY: What?

LUKE: Do you think that might send out a bad signal?

ANDY: What do you mean?

LUKE: If you turned up at a gig and there was a band called 'Out Of Tune' playing, would that fill you with confidence?

ANDY: That'd be funny. Out of Tune's funny.

LUKE: Fear Of Music is not a good name for a band.

ANDY: It is. You don't know shit anyway. It
           definitely is. You in tonight? I'm in
           tonight.

LUKE: I thought you were going out?

ANDY: No.

LUKE: Can you be out on Friday night?

ANDY: Why?

LUKE: I was going to have someone over. Mum's
           out.

ANDY: Who?

LUKE: You don't know her.

ANDY: Oh yeah?

LUKE: Don't start.

ANDY: I might know her.

LUKE: You won't.

ANDY: I might know her in the dark.

LUKE: You fucking don't.

ANDY:	What have you done with her? What?

LUKE:	Shut up.

ANDY:	Oh, you want her so much! Aw, sweet...

LUKE:	Look just be out Friday night!

ANDY:	Aww, cross. Aren't you? Aren't you cross?
	Aren't you cross? Can I come back later?

LUKE:	Obviously, yes. But stay out till eleven, all
	right?

ANDY:	Just remember the five stations, young
	Luke.

LUKE:	What are you talking about?

ANDY:	The stations of the chase. Find em, follow
	em, finger em, fuck em, forget em. I want
	you at three at least all right?

LUKE:	You are so odd.

ANDY:	Oh, you are so red. Where's Mum?

LUKE:	I don't know, she was out when I got
	back.

ANDY plays.

ANDY: What's her name?

LUKE: Fuck off.

ANDY: I bet you'll moan it in your sleep. I bet I'll
               know by the morning.

LUKE: Fuck off.

ANDY: I bet you're terrified.

LUKE: No.

ANDY: Just -

LUKE: What?

ANDY: Well.

LUKE: What?

ANDY: You know.

LUKE: What?

ANDY: Try not to come too quick.

5

LUKE: We'd go over on Sundays. Cross the bridge under the trainers hanging from the phone line, through Munnings Court down Artists Way and over the lakes. Walk as far as the back lake then set up in clear space. There were always hardcore there with tents who'd camped out Saturday. Radios and the Sunday football on, Radio One, tea in flasks and food they'd taken to last a weekend though they were only half a mile from their houses. When it all stops spinning I go through his things. I don't realise it's weird until I've started then I carry on anyway. In the cupboard, what used to be our cupboard but is now just his, there's a shoe box full of tapes with his writing on them. Top forties. It's only the last few months, but it's very consistent. He's doing it every Sunday afternoon. I put one on, on my old cassette player. I don't know why I didn't take it with me.

6

Night. LUKE is in bed reading the liner notes to a cassette. The cassette is playing. Enter ANDY.

ANDY: All right.

LUKE: All right.

ANDY: What you listening to?

LUKE: I'll switch it off.

ANDY: You don't have to.

LUKE: No, it's all right. [*LUKE switches off the cassette.*]

ANDY: So did you?

LUKE: What?

ANDY: I bet you didn't. I bet I've just spent the whole evening freezing in the park for nothing.

LUKE: Have you been in the park?

ANDY: Yeah. Why?

LUKE: Why didn't you go to the cinema or
           something? Why didn't you go to the pub?

ANDY: Because I went to the park. You didn't,
           did you. Tosser. It's a beautiful night.
           Look out the window.

LUKE: Leave it, the rail'll come down.

ANDY: I thought you fixed it?

LUKE: Only with short nails, it's weak. Leave it!

ANDY: All right! All right. I'm leaving the
           curtains. I'm sitting down on the bed. I'm
           undoing the zip on my top. I'm leaning
           forward. I'm undoing my laces.

LUKE: You're being a retard. You don't normally
           bother with your laces.

ANDY: No. They're hard to get undone, actually.

LUKE: They're pulled so tight because you never
           undo them.

ANDY: How's that?

LUKE: They stretch when you pull them off over
           your feet.

ANDY: I'm terrible with shoes. Tread the backs down too, look at that. [*Holds them up.*] That's because I don't bother with the laces too, I guess.

LUKE: Yeah.

ANDY: And I scuff the toes. How much room do you normally have in the end of your shoes?

LUKE: Not much, why?

ANDY: Because I have wide feet I have a lot of room in the end. I scuff the toes of all my shoes because I think my foot ends at one place, but my shoe actually ends about an inch further on. So I get my angles to the ground wrong. Like a bad pilot. All my shoes only ever last me about six months.

LUKE: You only ever wear one pair at a time, that's why they wear out.

ANDY: I only ever have one pair at a time.

LUKE: You shouldn't really have an inch at the end, that's got to be too big for you. Are your feet really that wide?

ANDY: Yeah. Look.

ANDY raises a foot to show to LUKE.

LUKE: They look normal to me.

ANDY: No they don't, look.

ANDY raises both feet.

LUKE: I'm looking. I looked. They look like my feet.

ANDY: Show me.

LUKE: My feet?

ANDY: Yeah. Hold them both up.

LUKE: Hold them up?

ANDY: You know what I mean, lift them.

LUKE: All right.

LUKE lifts both his feet up in the air so the soles are pointing at ANDY. ANDY looks at them. ANDY gets onto the floor.

ANDY: Hang on.

LUKE: What?

ANDY: I've got to work this out. Yours look just
             like mine.

LUKE: Yeah, and I don't have wide feet.

ANDY makes a lunge for the soles of LUKE's feet.

LUKE: Fuck off! Get off me!

ANDY: All right, all right.

He stands. He lunges for LUKE's feet again.

LUKE: No, fuck off, stop it! You'll wake up Mum!

ANDY: Chicken.

LUKE: Idiot.

ANDY: Girl.

LUKE: Great comeback.

ANDY: There wasn't anything worth coming back
             at.

LUKE: Queer.

ANDY: How come you always have all the best
            lines?

LUKE: It's all those books I read.

ANDY: While I'm getting so fucked I can't spell
            'E' any more.

LUKE: You're a tragic case.

ANDY: I haven't been sober since I was nine.
            Some days I can't even see. I mistake
            people for dogs, and - piss on them.

LUKE: Do you piss on dogs?

ANDY: Only when I'm on smack.

LUKE: And you're on smack a lot.

ANDY: It's because my brother beat me as a child.

LUKE: Only because you had a mental age of five.

ANDY: That's perfectly normal for a five year old.
            I was in a fight tonight.

LUKE: You what?

ANDY: With this lad from Munnings Court. He

hangs out by the bridge and he tried to stop me crossing over. So I smacked him.

LUKE: You smacked him?

ANDY: Yeah.

LUKE: You couldn't smack a baby.

ANDY: I could. I'm not a kid, you know.

LUKE: No?

ANDY: There's stuff you don't know about me.

LUKE: Like what?

ANDY: I'm going to see Judas Priest in October.

LUKE: You what?

ANDY: Got my tickets tonight. Ian got them.

LUKE: You can't go to Judas Priest.

ANDY: Why not?

LUKE: Mum won't let you.

ANDY: She won't know.

LUKE: Man, you can't, you'll get murdered. I'll
            have to tell her.

ANDY: You won't.

LUKE: I will.

ANDY: You'd better not.

LUKE: I'll have to. You can't go. Where is it?

ANDY: Birmingham.

LUKE: How will you get there?

ANDY: Ian's brother's going to drive us.

LUKE: He's banned.

ANDY: He won't be by October.

LUKE: You're not going.

ANDY: You can't do anything about it, you won't
            be here.

LUKE: I don't care, I'll tell her, you can't go to
            Birmingham.

ANDY: You wouldn't.

LUKE: I will.

ANDY: Why?

LUKE: For your own good.

ANDY: You won't.

LUKE: I ought to.

ANDY: You won't.

LUKE: Watch your step. [*Silence.*] What size shoes do you wear then?

ANDY: Elevens.

LUKE: You're never an eleven.

ANDY: I bought them to grow into.

LUKE: You should wear shoes that fit. I'm a nine, you're not an eleven.

ANDY: Yeah, right.

LUKE: You ever been to Birmingham?

ANDY: No.

LUKE: You're in for a treat.

ANDY: When did you go to Birmingham?

LUKE: I haven't. I read about it. It's sad the
           places people have to live.

ANDY: You've never been.

LUKE: No, but it is though. Imagine.
           Birmingham. Imagine living there.

ANDY: It's probably all right.

LUKE: You wouldn't understand.

ANDY: Why not?

LUKE: You'll get it / when you're older.

ANDY: Get what?

LUKE: It's not even sad, you know, it's
           outrageous. We pay our taxes and they
           make us live in Birmingham.

ANDY: We don't live in Birmingham.

LUKE: No –

ANDY: You don't pay tax.

LUKE: I don't want to either. I remember one
               time Dad was driving us somewhere in the
               car, when we had that car, that 2CV with
               the gappy floor you could see the road
               through. You know, you got wet from
               below in the rain. I don't know where he
               was taking us, some holiday or whatever.
               We were in the back of the car and you
               were asking him questions and driving him
               mad. You know how little kids ask
               questions? Or every time you say
               something, little kids just say 'why'? And
               you were doing that, everything he told
               you you just said why, why, why. We
               stopped in this petrol station, and he said
               he had to fill up. And you asked him –

ANDY: Why?

LUKE: And he banged his head on the steering
               wheel and said, I'm losing the will to live
               here. And you said, we don't live here, we
               live in Andover.

They laugh.

ANDY: Where did you do her then?

LUKE: In your bed.

ANDY: Fuck off, I mean how. What did you do?

LUKE: You idiot.

7

LUKE: Because I made mix tapes. I made mix tapes, he went out. And now there's this shoe box, and at the bottom I find old tapes of mine with my writing on them, but counting up the ones on top I can tell he's been doing it months now. I want to ask him why. He never used to copy me. I had a red coat so he had a blue one. I liked the Incredible Hulk so he collected Spiderman. I was Asterix so he was Tintin. It went like that. We had different colour tooth brushes and he wore Y fronts and I wore boxers. And he never recorded anything off the radio, just like I never played an instrument or tried to write a song. I want to ask him what changed. I didn't. Did I?

8

ANDY is smoking.

LUKE: Are you actually smoking?

ANDY: I didn't know you were reading rocket science.

LUKE: Does Mum let you? In here?

ANDY: In a way.

LUKE: In a way?

ANDY: I do what I want. They're my lungs.

LUKE: It's her house.

ANDY: True. Mum doesn't come upstairs.

LUKE: Her bedroom's upstairs.

ANDY: True. She comes up to sleep.

LUKE: She must smell it on you. In the hall.

ANDY: I haven't asked. We don't talk that much.

LUKE: You don't talk.

ANDY: I just told you, she doesn't come upstairs.
           So I smoke if I want.

LUKE: She wouldn't want you to.

ANDY: You don't want me to.

LUKE: No. Why would you smoke?

ANDY: Everyone needs a hobby.

LUKE: You're being hostile today, aren't you?

ANDY: I know why she's dragged you back.

LUKE: No one's dragged me anywhere. I've come
           home.

ANDY: You never come home.

LUKE: Can we sit down? I haven't even got my
           coat off and we're fighting.

ANDY: You're on my turf.

LUKE: You what?

ANDY: It's all right. I've had enough of this
           anyway. [*He stubs out the cigarette and sits
           on a bed.*] There you go.

LUKE: That's my bed.

ANDY: No it's not, I moved.

LUKE: When?

ANDY: I don't know, weeks ago. I needed a change.

LUKE: What are you using this one for?

ANDY: Nothing. I use it as a table.

LUKE: So I'm sleeping on the table.

ANDY: Kind of. Although it's actually a bed.

LUKE: Great. [*He sits.*] So.

ANDY: Hello.

LUKE: How are you?

ANDY: Are we gonna do small talk first?

LUKE: There's no first, I've just come back to see you. Yes, we're gonna do small talk.

ANDY: All right. I'm fine thanks, how are you?

LUKE: Fine. How's school?

ANDY: Fine. How's uni?

LUKE: Fine. What are you doing?

ANDY: I'm being civil.

LUKE: I don't mean now. You're just being a dick
            now. Mum's so upset, Andy.

ANDY: You'd think I'd committed a crime.

LUKE: It'll be the stupidest thing you've ever
            done.

ANDY: It'll be the only thing I've ever done. See,
            I haven't got a fucking hope if I don't,
            right? Of a fucking, proper - I'm not like
            you. I'm not clever like you. I'm not like
            you. And I want – you know? So what am
            I supposed to do?

LUKE: You could have talked to us.

ANDY: Are you a team now? Coupled up?

LUKE: Fuck off.

ANDY:	I will fuck off. That's exactly what I'm doing.
LUKE:	Why did you leave school?
ANDY:	There was no point in staying.
LUKE:	Of course there was.
ANDY:	She's got you here. She's got you here to inspire me back, you know that?
LUKE:	I'm not running errands.
ANDY:	You're doing her fucking weekly shop.
LUKE:	That's not how it is.
ANDY:	No, that's not what she's said. You think you're doing this off your own bat, but you're not, this is her idea. It's typical Mum tactics.
LUKE:	Tactics?
ANDY:	It's war in here. Didn't you know that?
LUKE:	Jesus. You're a mess.
ANDY:	I'm a mess because in eighteen years I've

never had the chance to express a thought of my own. Never. I have always been somebody else's. At school, at home, I am enlisted. I have to get out.

LUKE: Then do what I did.

ANDY: Stay in school?

LUKE: I want you to get out of here, you know that?

ANDY: I'll buy it for now.

LUKE: Of course I do. But you're doing it wrong.

ANDY: You mean I'm doing it differently.

LUKE: Don't be so fucking difficult.

ANDY: You'd be fucking difficult if you still lived in Andover.

LUKE: Andover's a nice town.

ANDY: No it's not.

LUKE: Look, you're never going to be Dad.

ANDY: What?

LUKE: You're not him. You're not him. It's not
            honest.

ANDY: I don't want to be anyone, what are you
            talking about?

LUKE: I just think...

ANDY: I'm not trying to be - this is my life. I just
            want a life is all. I just want. I'm not
            joining up because of Dad. I'm joining up
            for me, this is my thing.

LUKE: I don't believe you. You don't believe
            yourself either, you know you don't.

ANDY: What's so wrong with joining the army?

LUKE: You know that. We have specific reasons.

ANDY: No, we have prejudices. That's all this
            family has. I'm proud of him, I wouldn't
            mind being like him.

LUKE: They don't care about you, you know.
            They want their five years, they don't care
            any more than anyone else.

ANDY: You're displaying your prejudices.

LUKE: These are facts, you shit. Facts. That's
             how it works. What percentage of the
             drunks and homeless you see on the street
             do you think are ex army? Fucking most
             of them. It's a killing machine, it kills
             people. It does different people at different
             speeds, but that's what it does. You're
             making the wrong decision.

ANDY: You're a joke. Look at you with your
             serious face on. Will you chill out?

LUKE: What do you mean, chill out?

ANDY: It's just boring, banging on about fucking
             soldier's rights. Pension provision for the
             dog-walkers! Give clowns a living wage!
             What does it matter to you?

LUKE: It matters to me.

ANDY: It doesn't though, does it, and you don't
             do anything about it, and if you tried you
             couldn't, so why are you boring the arse
             off me?

LUKE: Fucking hell Andy.

ANDY: 'Fucking hell Andy.'

LUKE: Don't copy me. DON'T –say that back.

ANDY: So what, have you come all the way here just to talk about this?

LUKE: I can come home when I want, can't I?

ANDY: You never seem to want to though, do you.

LUKE: What does that mean?

ANDY: You never come home.

LUKE: It's very painful for me, coming back to Andover.

ANDY: You what?

LUKE: It's – I don't want to talk about it.

ANDY: It's very painful for you? That's the sort of thing Mum would say.

LUKE: No –

ANDY: 'It's too upsetting for me to go into Woolworths. My nerves are too bad.'

LUKE: No –

ANDY: 'I think of your little faces and everything I could have done and it's just too upsetting for me to get on a bus.' Jesus.

LUKE: It's about Sally, isn't it.

ANDY: Who's Sally?

LUKE: You know who Sally is. My ex.

ANDY: Did you break up?

LUKE: You remember who she is then!

ANDY: Now I think of it, yeah. You broke up?

LUKE: A year ago.

ANDY: Oh. Well.

LUKE: What do you mean, well?

ANDY: You could see that coming a mile off.

LUKE: What do you mean?

ANDY: Mate, you lived in different cities. What do you mean it's too upsetting for you to come home?

LUKE: I loved her, Andy. And I see her wherever I look round here.

ANDY: Oh fuck off!

LUKE: What –

ANDY: You were wandering round here a long time before you started getting noshed off by Sally. Fuck off you see her wherever you look. You just didn't fancy coming home.

LUKE: No.

ANDY: You've forgotten about this, I knew you would.

LUKE: I haven't.

ANDY: Don't you feel guilty? A little bit guilty you're off living and I'm still here? [*Silence*]. I do all right mind. Rule the roost. There's a kid across the bridge thinks he's harder than me, but he doesn't try anything. Just gets in my way when I try to go out to the lakes. Follows me round sometimes. I don't mind about him. I've got my 309, I've got my music. It's just a shame I'm living in a shit-hole.

LUKE: It's not.

ANDY: Grow up.

LUKE: You grow up.

ANDY: I'm done with this. I'm going out.

LUKE: I only just got here.

ANDY: I'm bored of you. I'm going out.

9

LUKE is recording the top forty. Trays of cassettes all round him.

ANDY: You at it again?

LUKE: Problem?

ANDY: Every bloody Sunday.

LUKE: It's only a hobby, everyone needs one.

ANDY: Yeah, you need one, you're weird.

LUKE: The biggest challenge is in beating the DJs.

ANDY: What?

LUKE: They talk over the ends of every song, to stop you recording them. So you go out and buy the single. You have to be clever, and guess when they're going to do it, and stop the tape before they talk. That's the game.

ANDY: The game?

LUKE: It's fun.

ANDY: You're mental.

LUKE: There's real skill to it. The more you get to
               know a DJ, the more it feels like you're
               really playing with them. Like chess. You
               try to work out each other's tricks and
               habits. Every week, I feel like I get better
               at knowing what he's going to do. Some
               weeks he doesn't get on the tape once.

ANDY: Do you listen to them once they're done?

LUKE: The tapes?

ANDY: Yeah.

LUKE: Yeah.

ANDY: Not when I'm here.

LUKE: I do it when you're out.

ANDY: Yeah, right.

Silence.

LUKE: I think a bird flew into the window this
               morning.

ANDY: Really?

LUKE: Yeah. I was recording, and I heard this
             bang. When I looked up I couldn't see
             anything, but there are marks on the
             window like wings. You'd probably find it
             if you looked in the hedge. I missed a song
             ending looking at it, Bruno Brooks got,
             like, fifteen words in.

ANDY: Did it die?

LUKE: Well if it didn't it's pretty fucking hard.

ANDY: Ian says he headbutted a kestrel once.

LUKE: You what?

ANDY: He was on his motorbike and it flew right
             in front of him. He couldn't stop. So he
             nutted it.

LUKE: He didn't actually nut it though did he.

ANDY: Why not?

LUKE: Well he just drove into it with his head,
             that's different. Just because it was his
             head doesn't mean it was a headbutt.

ANDY: It was a headbutt.

LUKE: Whatever.

ANDY: He says his uncle punched a mallard to
           death.

LUKE: Seriously?

ANDY: Yeah. He was driving along one day with
           his arm out the car window like this, and a
           duck flew into his fist.

LUKE: Again, that's not a punch. That's just
           driving into an animal.

ANDY: He punched a mallard to death. I killed a
           badger once.

LUKE: What?

ANDY: I was cycling, and I'd just written this
           really wicked song.

LUKE: Oh yeah.

ANDY: No, it was really wicked. Like, really
           wicked. And I was freewheeling down this
           hill singing the chorus, you know, to get
           the chorus right, and because it was really
           wicked, and these three badgers ran out in
           front of me. I hit the first two on the nose

and missed the third one. Didn't come off my bike, I was like, waay, like – wobbling and braking. Second badger I hit got up and ran off. But the first one, I'd broken its neck. It was thrashing its arse on the road like this. [*He mimes a badger with a broken neck dying.*] I went back to it, and I picked up a stick, because you're meant to finish them off. But like, badgers are well hard and theirs jaws lock when they bite, so I couldn't stamp on it or anything, so I got a stick. And by the time I got back to it, it had stopped thrashing, it was just breathing really heavily. I stood over it, and watched it breathe, and then it took this really big breath and I thought, that's it's last breath. And it was either like it was trying to get enough to keep living. Or like it was saying goodbye. And then its eyes went blank.

LUKE: Fucking hell.

ANDY: I got it off the road with the stick and next time I went past someone had moved it.

LUKE: I chucked a swan in a river.

ANDY: Yeah?

LUKE: It was dead on the bank. And I thought it
            would want to go back in the water, go
            home like. So I picked it up and I forgot to
            hold its neck so its neck broke. Then I
            chucked it in the river. And its neck got
            snagged on a branch. You've stopped
            practising.

ANDY: I had to give it back.

LUKE: To Ian?

ANDY: Yeah. He needs to practise.

LUKE: Do you know anyone else you can borrow
            one off?

ANDY: No. He's got to take it back though, or he
            can't practise.

LUKE: How do you rehearse?

ANDY: What?

LUKE: How do you play together, if you haven't
            got enough guitars?

ANDY: Well we don't yet, do we? We're just
            planning at the moment. We can't
            rehearse till I get a guitar.

LUKE: Mum might lend you the money.

ANDY: Don't be stupid, I wouldn't ask her. I'm so aware of it, all the time, money. How much I've got.

LUKE: I know.

ANDY: Do you think about it?

LUKE: Of course. I haven't got any.

ANDY: You don't like talking to me, do you?

LUKE: What?

ANDY: You stop when we talk about anything serious.

LUKE: So would anyone.

ANDY: I wish they didn't. I get bored staying quiet.

LUKE: It's nice sometimes.

ANDY: Not when there's this much going on in your head. I might join the army.

LUKE: You won't.

ANDY: Why not?

LUKE: You'll get shot.

ANDY: Probably. Knowing my luck.

LUKE: You'd be a crap shot.

ANDY: I'm a good paintballer.

LUKE: I'm better.

ANDY: When we went paintballing you were still
           a head taller than me. I reckon I'd beat
           you now.

LUKE: No way.

ANDY: I would.

LUKE: You out today?

ANDY: Where would I go on a Sunday?

LUKE: Out.

ANDY: No. That girl rang for you.

LUKE: Who?

ANDY: Sally.

LUKE: When?

ANDY: When you went out this morning.

LUKE: Did she say anything?

ANDY: She said she'd call back later. Have you
           fallen out?

LUKE: No.

ANDY: Sounded like it.

LUKE: I'm just not bothering. It's not worth it, is
           it? I'm leaving, aren't I, so there's no point
           in all - that. Not when I'm on my way out.
           So I haven't called her. I thought she
           wouldn't mind.

ANDY: She sounded like she minded.

LUKE: She shouldn't. Nothing happened, we just
           talked. I don't know why she's calling, I
           haven't called her.

ANDY: She said she'd maybe call this afternoon.

LUKE: Did she say when?

ANDY: No.

Silence.

LUKE: I might go for a walk.

ANDY: You can't just avoid her.

LUKE: I can. D'you wanna come?

ANDY: What? For a walk?

LUKE: Yeah.

ANDY: When did we ever go for a walk?

LUKE: I'm just asking.

ANDY: You're all right.

Silence

ANDY: Are you going then?

LUKE: I'll go in a minute.

ANDY: Mum's gone to church.

LUKE: No she hasn't, she went this morning.

ANDY: She's just gone, I passed her in the street.

LUKE: Did she say she was going to church?

ANDY: No, it's Sunday.

LUKE: Church is in the morning. How was she dressed?

ANDY: Normal.

LUKE: Normal, or normal for Mum?

ANDY: Well she didn't have her hair in rollers or anything, she looked all right.

LUKE: Which way was she going?

ANDY: Why?

LUKE: Will you change the tape over when it runs out?

ANDY: You're not going after her, are you?

LUKE: I want to see where she's gone. Was she heading for town?

ANDY: Yeah, but you ought to leave her alone, she's all right.

LUKE: I just want to check. She doesn't go out
              without saying goodbye. Will you change
              the tape over?

ANDY: All right.

LUKE: Will you?

ANDY: Yes.

10

LUKE: When was the last time you changed these sheets?

ANDY: Why?

LUKE: I went seven weeks last term without changing mine. Didn't think of it. I don't want to sleep in your old sheets if you haven't changed them.

ANDY: Can't you sleep downstairs?

LUKE: This is still my room.

ANDY: We'll both sleep better if you go downstairs.

LUKE: I won't. I can't sleep on sofas.

ANDY: Fine.

They undress for bed.

LUKE: My eyes are bloodshot.

ANDY: You should sleep more.

LUKE: And I should moisturize.

ANDY: Really?

LUKE: It's good for the skin.

ANDY: I have bad skin.

LUKE: I know, I saw. Do you feel embarrassed saying things like that?

ANDY: Why?

LUKE: It's just weird the stuff you talk about. You don't mind talking to me.

ANDY: No. You've lost weight.

LUKE: Do you think?

ANDY: I don't know. You haven't gained any. And people gain weight at uni, don't they, so in a way you've lost some.

LUKE: I suppose so.

ANDY: I have a lot more time since you left. I didn't think we did that much together, but there's loads of spare time now.

LUKE: Are you still in the band?

ANDY: You're really out of the loop, aren't you. I
               haven't been in the band for ages. I was
               never any good, you know that.

LUKE: No one's any good when they start.

ANDY: I tried pretty hard for a year. I'm sorry I
               was rough about that girl.

LUKE: You're all right.

ANDY: No, I'm sorry. I shouldn't have been –

LUKE: It's not really a thing.

ANDY: No?

LUKE: Yeah, I'll move on.

ANDY: Do you want the bathroom first?

LUKE: No, you have it.

ANDY: All right. Back in a minute.

*ANDY exits. LUKE looks around the room. ANDY comes
back in.*

LUKE: I've forgotten how to do this, it's
               awkward, isn't it.

ANDY: Share a room?

LUKE: Share anything. I'll be back in a minute.

Exit LUKE. ANDY looks around the room. Enter LUKE.

LUKE: Shall we go to bed then?

ANDY: All right.

LUKE turns the light off. They get into bed.

LUKE: How did it happen?

ANDY: I was getting a bus, and this bloke in uniform said to me that I'd make a good soldier. I suppose I was flattered. I thought about it for a bit, and then I went and did some research, and then I went and got the forms.

LUKE: Before or after you quit school?

ANDY: Same day, on the way home. I planned it all out.

LUKE: And you really want to do it?

ANDY: Yeah.

LUKE: You're mad, d'you know that?

ANDY: Maybe.

LUKE: He was playing on your weaknesses. Your
             pride. It's so dishonest.

ANDY: What is?

LUKE: They take advantage of how we live. See
             an unhappy kid, make him feel confident.
             See someone from this estate, tell them
             about the travel.

ANDY: I bet I'm stronger than you now.

LUKE: Oh yeah?

ANDY: I bet I am.

LUKE: Good for you.

ANDY: Do you want to try?

LUKE: Not really.

ANDY: Come on, losers don't try. Arm wrestle.

LUKE: No.

ANDY: Challenge. [*He gets out of bed and puts the*
               bin upside down on the floor in the middle of
               the stage.] Don't be a wuss.

LUKE: I'm not a wuss, I'm tired.

ANDY: You know you'd lose.

LUKE: I wouldn't.

ANDY: You're going to try.

LUKE: I'm not.

ANDY: You are. [*Silence.*] You are.

11

LUKE takes his coat off. He sits down to take off his shoes.
Night.

ANDY: All right?

LUKE: All right.

ANDY: What time is it?

LUKE: I don't know.

Silence.

ANDY: She got back about half an hour after you
                left. She went shopping. She cooked for
                you.

LUKE: Did you tell her I was sorry?

ANDY: Yes. And I said good night to her for you.

LUKE: You know what? I'm not sorry. I wouldn't
                have said good night.

ANDY: She was sad.

LUKE: It doesn't matter what she thinks, she
                can't do anything.

ANDY: You're pissed.

LUKE: No, I mean it. I don't have to be home for her.

ANDY: Where have you been?

LUKE: Walking.

ANDY: Drinking.

LUKE: Drinking and walking. And now I'm going to bed. [*Gets into bed. Silence.*] I walked out as far as where Dad used to work. I thought it might be like saying goodbye. It wasn't, it was a waste of time, I got a bus back. Then I went to the pub. And when the pub shut I went to Sally's. I shouldn't have really, too pissed. But we talked for a bit. And we made up. It was nice. I'm going to come back and see her some weekends. She's going to come up to London sometimes too. We're going to give it a go. [*Silence.*] What did you do today?

ANDY: Nothing. I played the guitar. I went for a walk.

LUKE: We might have bumped into each other.

ANDY: Yeah.

Silence.

LUKE: She's very beautiful, you know. I'll get a
               photo, you'd like her. Listens to you. It's
               nice to find someone like that. Someone
               you can just talk to, and not have to think
               about what you're talking about. It's nice
               just to talk, isn't it? If you can find the
               right person. I told her about Dad. I'd
               never told anyone that before. What are
               you going to do when I go?

ANDY: Dunno.

LUKE: Are you gonna be all right? [*Silence.*] Did
               you change that tape over?

ANDY: What?

LUKE: Did you change the tape over when it
               finished?

ANDY: Yeah.

Silence.

LUKE: You didn't, did you?

ANDY: I was downstairs talking to Mum. When I got back up it had already stopped. I thought I had ten minutes left, I was only gone for two or three.

Silence.

LUKE: Right.

12

LUKE: Are you really going to go?

ANDY: Yes.

LUKE: You're hurting her so much.

ANDY: She should come up here and tell me then.

LUKE: You can't let that be a reason. You don't talk either.

ANDY: I used to try. Do you love her?

LUKE: She's my Mum.

ANDY: Do you love her?

LUKE: Yes.

ANDY: So do I. That's the problem, isn't it. I should be packing.

LUKE: Don't pack.

ANDY: Why not? Would you really rather I stayed here, and you had to fish me out of the river another year down the line?

LUKE: You'd get on all right.

ANDY: I don't know. Would I?

LUKE: Will you give it a week?

ANDY: Before what?

LUKE: Before you make up your mind. For me.

ANDY: Why?

LUKE: So I know you've really thought about it?

ANDY: I have thought about it.

LUKE: If I beat you in an arm wrestle, will you
             give it a week?

ANDY: No!

LUKE: You wanted to last night.

ANDY: That was last night.

LUKE: If you beat me, you can do what you
             want. Go on.

ANDY: It's stupid.

LUKE gets the bin and turns it upside down.

LUKE: Come on.

ANDY: I'll beat you.

LUKE: Let's see you then.

ANDY: All right.

They kneel down opposite one another, pulling up trousers, getting their balance right. They link hands.

LUKE: Right.

ANDY: You'll lose.

LUKE: On three?

ANDY: OK.

LUKE: One. Two. Three.

13

LUKE is recording the top forty. ANDY opens the door and stands in the doorway.

ANDY: You told her. I've already paid for the ticket.

LUKE: You can't go.

ANDY: I can't believe you actually told her.

LUKE: It's for your own good. I couldn't let you go.

ANDY walks across the room. The cassettes are out. He stamps on a box of cassettes, four times. Turns to look at LUKE.

LUKE switches off the radio.

LUKE: I suppose someone needed to do that. It was a stupid habit.

ANDY: Fuck off.

LUKE: I'm sorry. It's for the best.

ANDY: Don't be fucking calm!

LUKE: Calm down.

ANDY: I could fucking scream at you.

LUKE: You should.

ANDY: I will.

LUKE: Sit down, Mum'll come up.

ANDY: I can't believe you.

LUKE: You should calm down.

ANDY: I am calm.

LUKE: Calm down.

ANDY: Don't talk to me.

LUKE: That's what we always get to, isn't it. You telling me to shut up.

ANDY: I don't want to hear you.

LUKE: It's not healthy.

ANDY: No, it's not.

LUKE: I did it for your own good.

ANDY: You're ridiculous, you know that? You're
           ridiculous. Just cos I didn't do your
           fucking tape.

LUKE: That's not –

ANDY: Fuck off, it is. Just cos I messed up your
           stupid fucking game. You're such a such a
           – Christ!

Silence.

LUKE: You'll probably do better when I'm out of
           the way. [*Silence.*] I need to get the
           suitcases out of the loft.

ANDY: Are you packing already?

LUKE: Got to start some time, haven't I.

ANDY: How are you getting there?

LUKE: Mr Johnson's driving me.

ANDY: Can I come?

LUKE: There isn't room. [*Silence.*] You'll go as
           well, in a year or two.

ANDY: I won't.

LUKE: Why not?

ANDY: I might move out, but I won't go.
             Someone's got to look after Mum forever
             now. She's got no friends, so it has to be
             me.

LUKE: I'm not going for ever.

ANDY: Yeah, but it hasn't crossed your mind, has
             it? You haven't thought about it once.
             You'll go, and she'll end up trying to kill
             herself or something, and you'll get the
             first train back and take over, and take the
             credit for sorting her out, but by then the
             hard bit will have happened. It'll be me
             that calls you. It'll be me that stops in
             every day, and eats with her, and has her
             round for Christmas.

LUKE: I'll do my bit.

ANDY: How can you? It'll be me she ends up
             living with, not you.

LUKE: We don't know that. *[Silence]* Andy look.
             Look at me. Andy look at me.

14

Night. ANDY and LUKE are in bed. ANDY is crying and whimpering.

LUKE: Andy. Are you awake, can you hear me?

ANDY: It's not fair that I'm going to get Mum and you get to fuck off somewhere else.

LUKE: You're awake.

ANDY: Yeah.

LUKE: I thought you were asleep again.

ANDY: What are you talking about?

LUKE: I thought you were sleepwalking.

ANDY: I don't sleepwalk.

LUKE: Yeah you do. You walk around and I put you back into bed.

ANDY: Fuck off do I.

LUKE: You do.

ANDY: Yeah? Why haven't you told me before?

LUKE: I didn't realise you didn't know.

ANDY: Bollocks.

LUKE: I put you back into bed, like, one night
           every three.

ANDY: Bollocks. You've never thought to wake
           me up? Bollocks.

LUKE: No it's not. It's been happening for three
           years, you know it has. [*Silence.*] You'll go
           as well, in a year or two.

ANDY: No I won't.

LUKE: Why not?

ANDY: I might move out, but I won't go.
           Someone's got to look after Mum forever
           now. She's got no friends, so it has to be
           me.

Silence.

LUKE: I'm not going for ever.

ANDY: Yeah, but it hasn't crossed your mind, has
           it? You haven't thought about it once.
           You'll go, and she'll end up trying to kill

86

herself or something, and you'll get the first train back and take over, and take the credit for sorting her out, but by then the hard bit will have happened. It'll be me that calls you. It'll be me that stops in every day, and eats with her, and has her round for Christmas.

LUKE: I'll do my bit.

ANDY: How can you? It'll be me she ends up living with, not you.

LUKE: We don't know that. [*Silence.*] You can't worry like this. You can't be sleep walking around once I'm not here.

ANDY: I don't sleep walk.

LUKE: You do.

ANDY: Then why didn't you tell me?

15

LUKE: When I opened the door I could see us ten years ago. I mean, real ghosts, I could hear us. And I'm sitting here now with this box of tapes on my lap, and I can smell him, but he's not here. Mum rang at half one and I got the first train. She couldn't speak. I didn't quite know for sure. I didn't know what – there wasn't anything to do. I sat on the train and counted the fields while they cleaved open like ham off the bone. It got dark so early. This is where we slept. . I can't help thinking, was this me? Was I supposed to stay, was it me did this to him? Or why do I feel so guilty?

16

LUKE and ANDY are packing.

ANDY: I've read this one.

LUKE: He's good, isn't he?

ANDY: Yeah.

LUKE: Do you want to put something on?

ANDY: What? Oh right.

LUKE: Pick something you like.

ANDY looks through the tapes.

ANDY: Will you call when you get there?

LUKE: Of course. Once I've unpacked.

ANDY: You should go and meet the other people
              on the corridor first, as well.

LUKE: I'll call first. There'll probably be drinks or
              something later.

They finish packing.

LUKE: I think that's everything.

ANDY: We can bring anything you forget up,
                 anyway.

LUKE: And I'll be back on Saturday.

ANDY: Yeah.

LUKE: What?

ANDY: You should stay away. Once you're out,
                 you should enjoy it.

LUKE: We'll see. [*Silence.*] What are you going to
                 do tonight?

ANDY: Oh, you know.

LUKE: No. Have you got anything to do?

ANDY: Of course.

LUKE: What?

ANDY: Nothing.

LUKE: Come on.

Silence.

ANDY: I'll go twitching till it gets dark.

LUKE: Seriously?

ANDY: Yeah.

LUKE: Really?

LUKE finds this next speech upsetting.

ANDY: Where do you think I go when I go out?
               Do you think I've got the money to be
               drinking all that time? There's a hide in
               the park at the end of the road, and a
               feeder. You can watch that. I can sit there
               for hours. At the weekend I walk out to
               the big lake, the ducks and the geese stop
               there when they're migrating. You can see
               dozens of species there.

LUKE: I didn't know you did this. I didn't know
               about this.

ANDY: It's only a hobby.

They look at each other. They look away.

17

The door bursts open and ANDY rushes in. He slams the door shut behind him and leans against it. He is desperately out of breath. He goes to the window and looks out. He changes out of his clothes and puts on new ones. He stands on the bed to look out of the window. He sits down on the bed and holds himself.

18

LUKE launches himself at ANDY, trying to pin him to the floor. ANDY tries to fight him off. Eventually LUKE gets him in a headlock. They stop. They breathe heavily.

LUKE: Talk.

ANDY: I don't want to.

LUKE: Talk, fucking talk, fucking talk!

ANDY: He was on the bridge and he wouldn't let me past him. Started talking about Dad. Your Dad's a fucking hobo, he'd rather the drink than your face every day. And I wasn't going to take it. I punched him till he wasn't moving then I think my head went and I chucked him off the bridge.

LUKE: Oh Christ.

ANDY: It's your fault.

LUKE: How is it my –

ANDY: You should have been here.

LUKE: I can't –

ANDY: You should have, anyway.

LUKE: Look -

ANDY: Is that them? Is that them, have they found me? How have they come so quick?

LUKE: They won't know it's you yet.

ANDY: Fuck. I've got thirty seconds. I've got thirty more seconds.

LUKE: You have to deny it. You can't tell them what you just said to me.

ANDY: That's what happened.

LUKE: You'll go to prison, you have to deny it.

ANDY: There were cars. They were swerving. I might as well say, it'll help. You know it will.

LUKE: Fuck. What were you thinking?

ANDY: I had to stick up for myself. I have to go downstairs now. Will you let me go?

LUKE: What if we went out the window?

ANDY: What?

LUKE: We could jump out the window, get on a
           train. We could go to London. We could
           get away.

ANDY: Come off it.

LUKE: Why not? We could hide, they wouldn't
           find us. We could go anywhere. We could
           hide.

ANDY: It's not a fucking film, Luke. You don't
           escape, right? It doesn't work like a movie.

LUKE: Oh my God.

ANDY: Will you let me up? I want to do my hair
           before I go.

Luke lets Andy up. Silence.

ANDY: I hate this room. It might be nice to get
           away for a while.

End.